Who Pooped

in the Park?

written by Gary D. Robson · illustrations by Elijah Brady Clark

FARCOUNTRY
PRESS

To my son, Douglas.

ISBN 10: 1-56037-280-X
ISBN 13: 978-1-56037-280-6

© 2004 by Farcountry Press
Text © 2004 by Gary D. Robson

For more information about our books, write Farcountry Press, P.O. Box 5630,
Helena, MT 59604; call (800) 821-3874; or visit www.farcountrypress.com.

Manufactured by:
Bolvo Yuanzhou Midas Printing Ltd.
Bolvo Yuanzhou Town Xianan Administration District
Huizhou, Guangdong
People's Republic of China
May 2012
Printed in China.

Created, produced, and designed in the United States.

16 15 14 13 12   4 5 6 7 8

"Dad? I have to go to the bathroom." Michael squirmed in the back seat.

"We'll be at our campground in just half an hour," said Dad.
"We're in Grand Teton National Park now."

"He's just nervous," said Michael's sister. "He thinks a bear's gonna eat him." She growled at Michael and made her fingers look like claws.

"Stop it, Emily," said Mom. "Nobody is getting eaten by anything."

4

Michael was very excited about the trip, but Emily was right. He was nervous. He had just read a book about grizzly bears. He knew how big they could get. He also knew that a hungry grizzly bear would eat just about anything—maybe even a boy.

"I *am* kind of scared of bears," admitted Michael.

"Don't worry," Dad told him. "We'll show you how to count a bear's toes and never get close enough to be scared."

"Here's our campsite. Let's set up the tent. Then we can go for a walk and I'll show you what I mean," Dad said. Michael was awfully worried about grizzly bear toes, but tried not to show it.

"Let's hurry!" said Emily. "I want to see some animals!"

Once the tent was up, the whole family went for a hike. Emily started to complain before they even left the campground. "I haven't seen any animals yet. Maybe there aren't any here!"

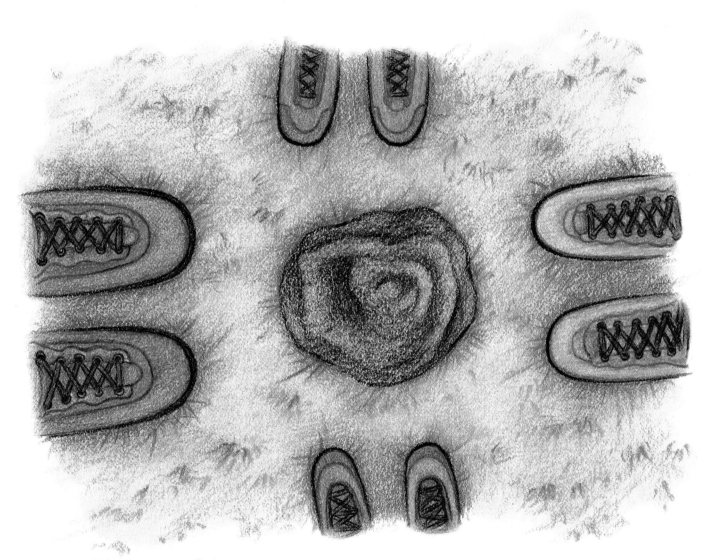

"There are definitely animals here," said Dad. "We're going to learn about them from their scat."

"Scat?" said Michael. "What's scat?"

"Scat is the word hikers and trackers use for animal poop," Mom said. "This big flat thing is bison poop. People call these buffalo chips."

When bison poop is dried out, it can be used in a campfire instead of wood. Plains Indians did this when there were no trees nearby.

"It looks hard," said Michael. "Not squishy like poop."

"Fresh bison poop *is* squishy," answered Dad. "But it dries out. You can tell how old it is by how hard it is."

American bison

water buffalo from India

cape buffalo from Africa

"Bison?" said Emily. "I thought Mom said this was from a buffalo."

"Technically, they're called bison," Dad responded. "But early settlers called them buffalo because they look like buffaloes from other parts of the world, and the name stuck."

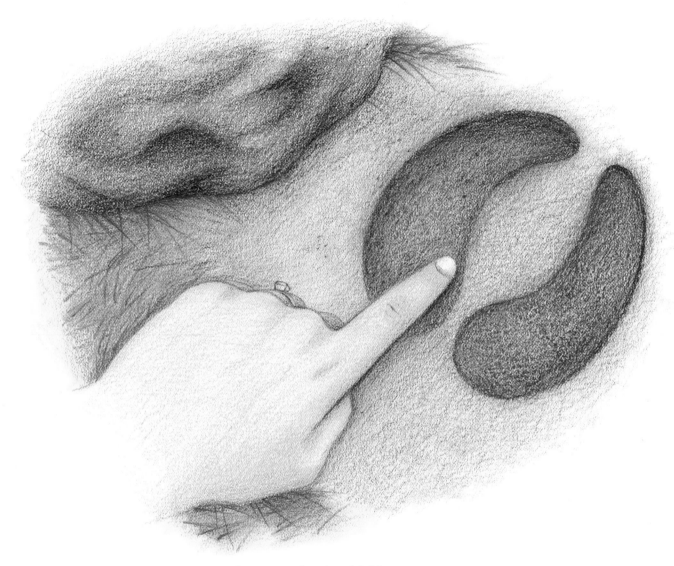

"Here are some bison tracks," said Mom.

"They have big feet," Emily giggled.

"Bison are the biggest animals in the Park," responded Dad.
"Males weigh as much as a small car."

"That's bigger than a grizzly bear!" said Michael.

"Look over here by the pond," said Mom.

"Footprints!" said Michael.

"And something else, too," added Mom. "Beaver scat."

"It looks like little pieces of wood," said Emily.

"Beavers gnaw on wood all the time," said Dad. "Their scat has lots of wood chips in it."

"They use the trees to build their dams and the lodges they live in," added Mom, "and they eat the bark."

15

"See, Michael," said Dad. "We don't have to get up close to an animal to learn about it. Instead of a close encounter of the *scary* kind, we'll have a close encounter of the *poopy* kind."

Everybody laughed, and Mom made a gross-out face.

"Dad! Mom! Look over here! I found bunny scat!" yelled Michael. "It's just like what we have in Fluffy's cage."

"We came all the way to Grand Teton National Park for *that?*" grumbled Emily. "Michael's bunny makes plenty of poop at home."

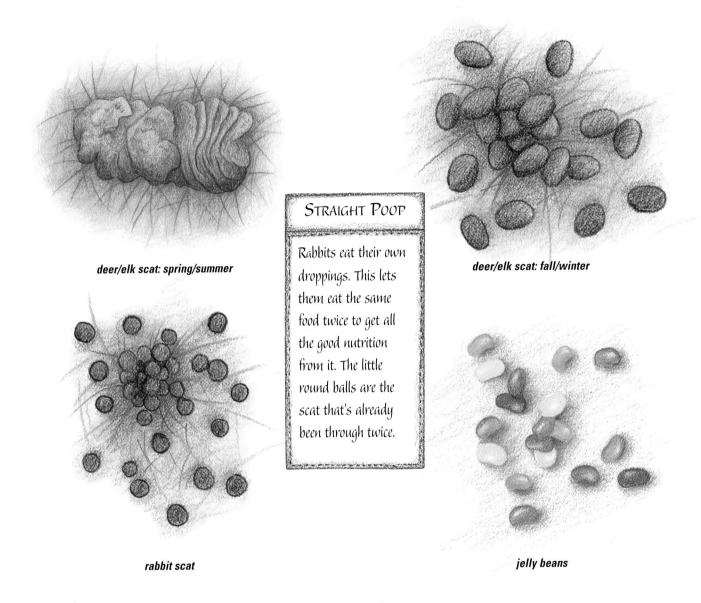

deer/elk scat: spring/summer

deer/elk scat: fall/winter

STRAIGHT POOP

Rabbits eat their own droppings. This lets them eat the same food twice to get all the good nutrition from it. The little round balls are the scat that's already been through twice.

rabbit scat

jelly beans

"That's not from a rabbit," said Mom, "It's from a deer."

"Right! Bunny poop looks like little round balls," added Dad. "Deer scat is shaped more like jelly beans."

"Are these deer tracks?" Michael asked.

"Yes!" said Mom. "See how they have split hooves?"

"Cool!" added Emily. She was starting to get interested.

"But what are these marks?"

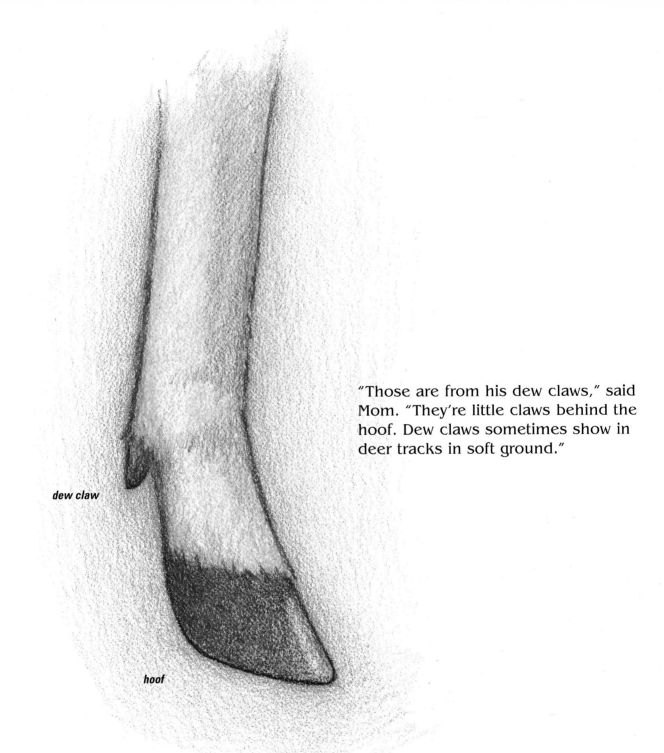

dew claw

hoof

"Those are from his dew claws," said Mom. "They're little claws behind the hoof. Dew claws sometimes show in deer tracks in soft ground."

20

STRAIGHT POOP

Sometimes mule deer bounce along with all four feet hitting the ground together. This is called "stotting" or "pronking."

"Oh, no!" said Michael. "Here's one of his antlers. Did a bear eat him?" Michael looked around nervously.

"No, he's fine. Deer and elk shed their antlers every winter and then grow a new, bigger set the next year. This antler is from an elk."

"This elk was in a hurry, though," said Mom, as she studied the ground.

Michael and Emily went over to look.

"How can you tell?" said Michael.

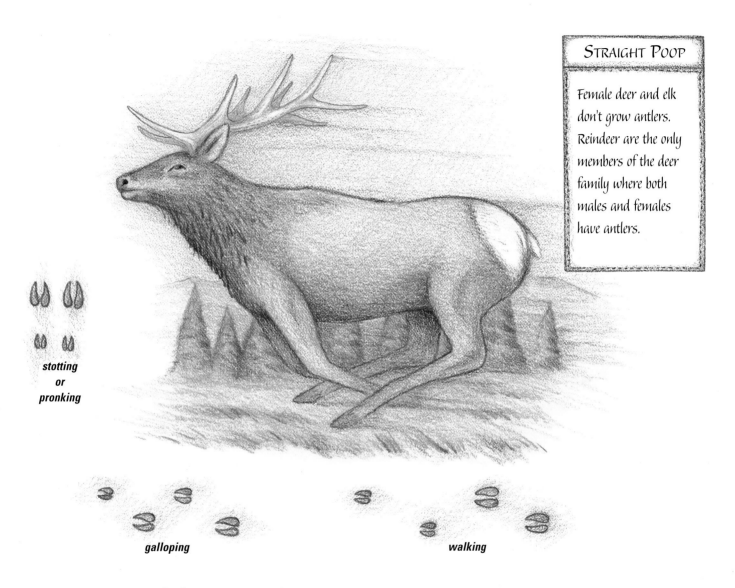

stotting or pronking

galloping

walking

"The hoofprints get very far apart here," Mom explained, "and the back prints are in front of the front prints."

"He was walking backwards?" said Emily.

"No, he was galloping. Something scared him and he was moving fast."

"I know what scared him," Dad called.

The family hurried over to look.

"This is coyote scat," Dad said, "and there are coyote tracks all around here."

"They look like dog tracks," said Michael.

"That's because coyotes are a member of the dog family," explained Dad.

25

"There were a lot of coyotes around here," said Mom.
"See how the tracks are different sizes?"

"Their den is probably nearby, and they scared the elk,"
Dad guessed.

"Did the coyotes get him?" Michael asked.

"I don't think so," said Mom. "Look!"

Far across the meadow, they saw a family of coyotes, lying in the sun.

"Wow! There's a huge pile right here in the middle of the trail."

"That's not from a coyote. All you can see in it are vegetables and something that looks like oats," said Dad.

"It's horse poop!" said Emily.

"Right," said Mom. "People ride horses out here. See if you can find any tracks."

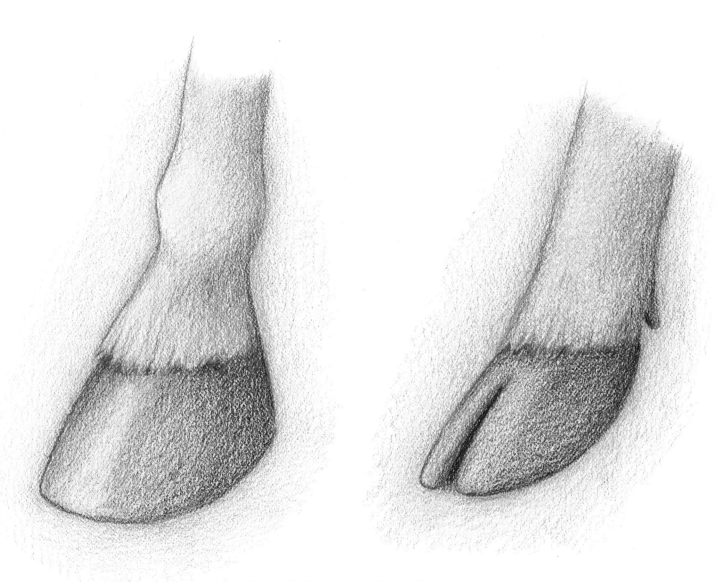

Michael found tracks, all right, but they didn't look like he expected.

"That's an awfully funny-shaped hoof," he said.

"Horses don't have split hooves like elk and deer," said Dad,
"It's just one part."

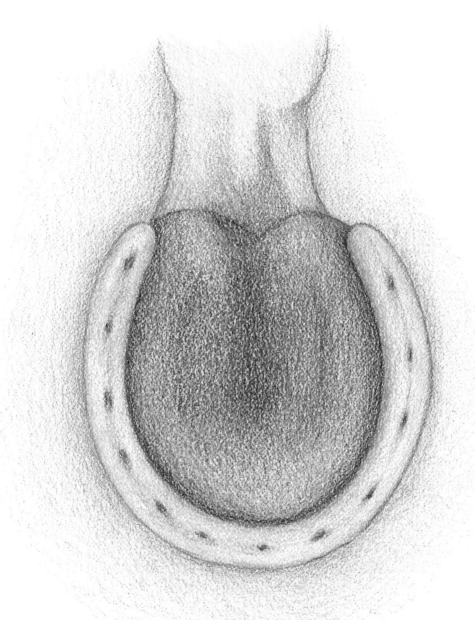

"He means the shoe," said Mom.

Michael looked puzzled and Dad laughed. "Horses that are ridden a lot have metal shoes to keep their hooves from wearing down. That's the track you're seeing."

"What are these tracks over here?" asked Emily. She was kneeling by a hole in the ground looking at some tracks.

Dad took a close look. "Check out those long claw marks, kids!"

"Is it from a bear?" Michael said with a shudder.

"No," said Dad. "These are badger tracks, and that's
the hole he lives in."

"His claws are huge," said Emily.

"That's how he digs the holes," Mom answered. "He uses those front feet and claws like shovels and picks."

Michael followed the tracks backward from
the hole and spotted some big hoofprints.

"I found more bison prints over here!"

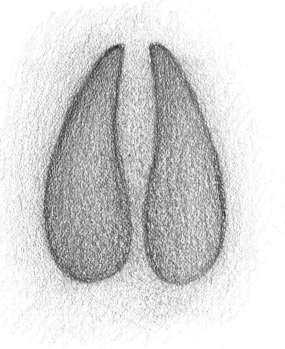

moose track

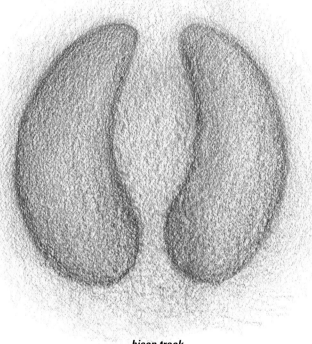

bison track

"Those aren't bison prints," Dad pointed out. "They're much pointier and not nearly as wide."

"Right," said Mom. "They're definitely moose tracks."

37

"Moose like to hang out near streams and lakes to eat water plants," said Dad, "but they come into the forests a lot, too."

"Whoa, Dad! What happened to this tree? Did an animal do that?"

"Something was sharpening its claws, Michael. And if you look how high those scratch marks go, it was pretty big!"

"It's not just the animal that's big," said Emily.
"Look at the size of this poop!"

"It looks like we found your grizzly bear," said Dad.
"Let's see what you learned today. What can you
figure out about this bear?"

"He's taller than you, and he has really long claws," said Michael.

"He's been eating plants," said Emily, "because there's no hair or bones in here."

"Good!" Mom said. "What else?"

STRAIGHT POOP

Grizzlies eat almost anything. They like fish and many kinds of plants, roots, and berries. Grizzlies can hunt their own meat, but they often steal kills away from wolves and other predators. They even eat moths and other insects.

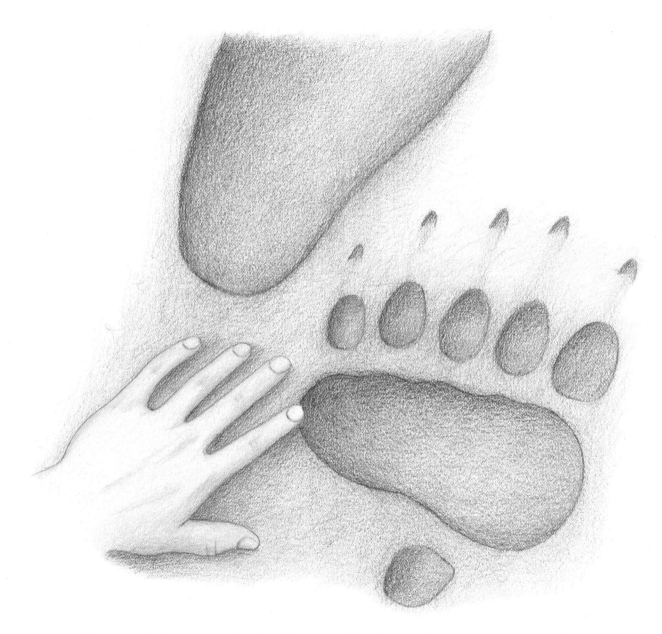

"Here's his footprint," said Michael. "It's huge! He has more toes than a coyote, and his claws are longer than my fingers."

"I told you you'd be able to count a grizzly's toes," laughed Dad.

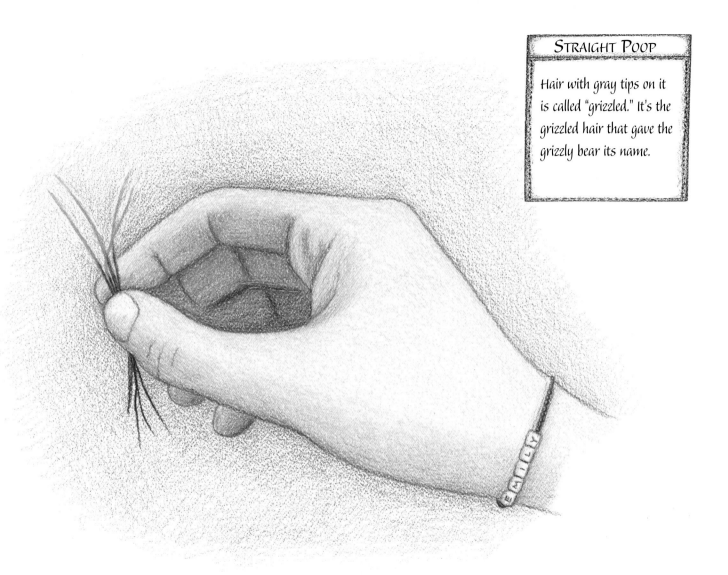

STRAIGHT POOP

Hair with gray tips on it is called "grizzled." It's the grizzled hair that gave the grizzly bear its name.

"He rubbed off some hair on the tree," said Emily. "It's really dark, but the tips are gray."

"Just like Dad's," smiled Mom.

"Don't pick on me," Dad grinned back.

As they ate dinner that night, everyone talked about how much fun they had.

"We didn't see very many animals," said Emily, "but it seemed like we did."

"And I didn't get scared once," said Michael.

Tracks and Scat Notes

Grizzly Bear
Very big tracks show large claw marks. Scat changes depending on diet. Claw marks show high on trees.

Rabbit
Small tracks filled in between toes. Scat is little balls.

Mule Deer
Pointy split-hoof tracks. Scat is long and oval-shaped like jelly beans, not round like a rabbit's.

Elk
Tracks are longer and more blunt than that of deer. Scat is quite a bit bigger than that of deer.

Horse
Tracks are almost as big as that of bison or elk, but wider and not split. Scat is in chunks, with roughage from vegetation often visible.

Moose
Tracks are bigger than that of elk and much pointier. Scat is a lot like that of elk.

Beaver
Tracks are large, with slender toes and webbed hind feet, often obscured by dragging tail marks. Scat is rarely found.

Coyote
Tracks are like dog prints, with claws showing. Scat usually tapers off in long tails, and often contains hair and bones.

Bison
Tracks are as long as moose tracks but much wider and blunt tipped. Scat looks like cow patties.

Badger
Tracks show very long front claws connected to the toes. Scat is rarely seen.

The Author

Gary Robson is a freelance writer who has written books for both children and adults as well as hundreds of magazine and newspaper articles. Gary is an expert in closed captioning technology for deaf people, and he has a teaching credential in computer science. He and his wife own a bookstore in Montana just outside Yellowstone National Park. For more about Gary, visit www.robson.org/gary.

The Illustrator

Elijah Brady Clark has been passionate about design and illustration for as long as he can remember. After living his dream of traveling the United States in an Airstream Bambi Travel Trailer, he returned to northwestern Montana's Flathead Valley, where he grew up. He currently works as a designer and illustrator.

BOOKS IN THE WHO POOPED IN THE PARK? SERIES:

Acadia National Park
Big Bend National Park
Black Hills
Colorado Plateau
Death Valley National Park
Glacier National Park
Grand Canyon National Park
Great Smoky Mountains National Park
Grand Teton National Park
Northwoods
Olympic National Park
Red Rock Canyon National Conservation Area
Rocky Mountain National Park
Sequoia and Kings Canyon National Parks
Shenandoah National Park
Sonoran Desert
Yellowstone National Park
Yosemite National Park